Answers to Questions About the National Flood Insurance Program

I0439981

FEDERAL EMERGENCY MANAGEMENT AGENCY

Addendum to
Answers to Questions About the NFIP

CLARIFICATION TO QUESTIONS 69 AND 70

The following questions and answers conform to current Standard Flood Insurance Policy wording.

69. What is flood in progress and how does it differ from the date of loss?

The date of loss is the date a flood, as defined in the Standard Flood Insurance Policy (SFIP), actually touches and damages NFIP-insured property. A loss caused by a flood in progress at the time an SFIP comes into effect may be subject to the flood-in-progress exclusion. If the SFIP was effective prior to the date the flood in progress began, coverage will be effective. A flood is in progress on the earlier of either the date the community in which the NFIP-insured property is located first experiences a flood as defined in the SFIP, or on the date of an event initiating a flood that directly or indirectly affects areas downstream or in a floodway.

70. Is damage caused by a flood in progress covered?

If a policy is in effect on the date the flood in progress begins, damage caused by the flood in progress is covered, subject to the terms of the SFIP. If a policy is effective after the date the flood is in progress, damage caused by the flood in progress most likely will not be covered. However, each NFIP claim is adjusted individually and the cause of any loss, and any applicable limitations or exclusion in the SFIP, is determined during the claims adjustment process.

Answers to Questions About the National Flood Insurance Program

This book is intended to acquaint the public with the National Flood Insurance Program (NFIP). Despite the highly technical nature of the Program, there has been a deliberate effort to minimize the use of technical terms. This publication is designed for readers who do not need a detailed history or refined technical or legal explanations, but who do need a basic understanding of the Program and the answers to some frequently asked questions. Readers who need legal definitions should refer to the Standard Flood Insurance Policy (SFIP) and to NFIP and related regulations.

The information provided herein is as current as possible, but changes in the NFIP are made periodically. Readers can obtain the most up-to-date insurance data by using the contact information at the back of the book.

The use of acronyms and initials has been limited, but some terms are used so often that acronyms are practical and helpful to the reader. Each term is spelled out upon its first use in the text, with the acronym or initials following in parentheses. For readers' convenience, the following is a list of acronyms and initials that appear in *Answers to Questions About the NFIP*:

BFE	Base Flood Elevation
CAP-SSSE	Community Assistance Program, State Support Services Element
CBIA	Coastal Barrier Improvement Act (of 1990)
CBRA	Coastal Barrier Resources Act (of 1982)
CBRS	Coastal Barrier Resources System
CLOMA	Conditional Letter of Map Amendment
CLOMR	Conditional Letter of Map Revision
CLOMR-F	Conditional Letter of Map Revision Based on Fill
CRS	Community Rating System
CTP	Cooperating Technical Partner
DFIRM	Digital Flood Insurance Rate Map
DHS	U.S. Department of Homeland Security
FEMA	Federal Emergency Management Agency
FHBM	Flood Hazard Boundary Map
FIRA	Flood Insurance Reform Act (of 2004)
FIRM	Flood Insurance Rate Map
FIS	Flood Insurance Study
FMA	Flood Mitigation Assistance Grant Program
FMIX	FEMA's Map Information eXchange
GFIP	Group Flood Insurance Policy

HMGP ....Hazard Mitigation Grant Program
ICC ....Increased Cost of Compliance
LODR ....Letter of Determination Review
LOMA ....Letter of Map Amendment
LOMC ....Letter of Map Change
LOMR ....Letter of Map Revision
LOMR-F ....Letter of Map Revision Based on Fill
NFIA ....National Flood Insurance Act (of 1968)
NFIP ....National Flood Insurance Program
NFIRA ....National Flood Insurance Reform Act (of 1994)
OPA ....Otherwise Protected Area
PDM ....Pre-Disaster Mitigation Grant Program
PMR ....Physical Map Revision
PRP ....Preferred Risk Policy
RCBAP ....Residential Condominium Building Association Policy
RFC ....Repetitive Flood Claims Grant Program
SDF ....Special Direct Facility
SFHA ....Special Flood Hazard Area
SFHDF ....Standard Flood Hazard Determination Form
SFIP ....Standard Flood Insurance Policy*
SRL ....Severe Repetitive Loss
WYO ....Write Your Own

* There are three Standard Flood Insurance Policy (SFIP) forms: The Dwelling Form SFIP, the General Property Form SFIP, and the Residential Condominium Building Association Policy SFIP. The SFIPs are available on the Web at http://www.fema.gov/business/nfip/sfip.shtm.

Contents

CONTENTS

Introduction to the NFIP

1. What is the National Flood Insurance Program (NFIP)?

The NFIP is a Federal program created by Congress to mitigate future flood losses nationwide through sound, community-enforced building and zoning ordinances and to provide access to affordable, federally backed flood insurance protection for property owners. The NFIP is designed to provide an insurance alternative to disaster assistance to meet the escalating costs of repairing damage to buildings and their contents caused by floods.

Participation in the NFIP is based on an agreement between local communities and the Federal Government that states that if a community will adopt and enforce a floodplain management ordinance to reduce future flood risks to new construction in Special Flood Hazard Areas (SFHAs), the Federal Government will make flood insurance available within the community as a financial protection against flood losses.

2. Why was the NFIP established by Congress?

For decades, the national response to flood disasters was generally limited to constructing flood-control works such as dams, levees, seawalls, and the like, and providing disaster relief to flood victims. This approach, however, did not reduce losses, nor did it discourage unwise development. In some instances, it may have actually encouraged additional development. To compound the problem, due to its high risk and seasonal nature, insurance companies were not able to provide affordable flood insurance coverage.

In light of mounting flood losses and escalating costs of disaster relief to the taxpayers, the U.S. Congress created the NFIP. The intent was to reduce future flood damage through community floodplain management ordinances, and provide protection for property owners against potential losses through an insurance mechanism that requires a premium to be paid for the protection.

3. How was the NFIP established and who administers it?

The U.S. Congress established the NFIP on August 1, 1968, with the passage of the National Flood Insurance Act (NFIA) of 1968. The NFIP was broadened and modified with the passage of the Flood Disaster Protection Act of 1973 and other legislative measures. It was further modified by the National Flood Insurance Reform Act (NFIRA) of 1994 and the Flood Insurance Reform Act (FIRA) of 2004. The NFIP is administered by the Federal Emergency Management Agency (FEMA), a component of the U.S. Department of Homeland Security (DHS).

4. What is a Special Flood Hazard Area (SFHA)?

In support of the NFIP, FEMA identifies flood hazard areas throughout the United States and its territories. Most areas of flood hazard are commonly identified on Flood Insurance Rate Maps (FIRMs). Areas not yet identified by a FIRM may be mapped on Flood Hazard Boundary Maps (FHBMs). Several areas of flood hazards are identified on these maps. One of these areas is the Special Flood Hazard Area (SFHA).

The SFHA is a high-risk area defined as any land that would be inundated by a flood having a 1-percent chance of occurring in a given year (also referred to as the base flood). The high-risk-area standard constitutes a reasonable compromise between the need for building restrictions to minimize potential loss of life and property and the economic benefits to be derived from floodplain development. Development may take place within an SFHA, provided that development complies with local floodplain management ordinances, which must meet the minimum Federal requirements. Flood insurance is required for insurable structures within high-risk areas to protect Federal financial investments and assistance used for acquisition and/or construction purposes within communities participating in the NFIP.

5. What is a Flood Insurance Rate Map (FIRM)?

A Flood Insurance Rate Map (FIRM) is an official map of a community on which FEMA has delineated both the special hazard areas and the risk premium zones applicable to the community.

6. What is a flood?

Flood is defined in the Standard Flood Insurance Policy (SFIP), in part, as:

> A general and temporary condition of partial or complete inundation of two or more acres of normally dry land area or of two or more properties (at least one of which is your property) from overflow of inland or tidal waters, from unusual and rapid accumulation or runoff of surface waters from any source, or from mudflow.

For a complete definition, refer to Section II. Definitions, A1 and A2 of the flood insurance policy.

7. What is the NFIP's Write Your Own (WYO) Program?

The Write Your Own (WYO) Program, begun in 1983, is a cooperative undertaking of the insurance industry and FEMA. The WYO Program allows participating property and casualty insurance companies to write and service Federal flood insurance policies in their own names.

Companies underwrite policies and process claims while the Federal Government retains responsibility for underwriting losses. All WYO Companies provide identical coverage, and rates are subject to NFIP rules and regulations.

8. Do state insurance regulators have any jurisdiction over the NFIP in their respective states?

As established by the U.S. Congress, the sale of flood insurance under the NFIP is subject to FEMA rules and regulations. FEMA has elected to have state-licensed insurance companies' agents and brokers sell flood insurance to consumers. State regulators hold the insurance companies' agents and brokers accountable for providing NFIP customers with the same standards and level of service that the states require of them in selling their other lines of insurance.

Private insurance companies participating in the Write Your Own (WYO) Program must be licensed and regulated by states to engage in the business of property insurance in those states in which they wish to sell flood insurance.

9. How does the NFIP benefit property owners? Taxpayers? Communities?

Through the NFIP, property owners in participating communities are able to insure against flood losses. By employing wise floodplain management, a participating community can reduce risk and protect its citizens and the community against much of the devastating financial losses resulting from flood disasters. Careful local management of development in the floodplains results in construction practices that can reduce flood losses and the high costs associated with flood disasters to all levels of government.

10. What is the definition of a community?

A community, as defined for the NFIP's purposes, is any state, area, or political subdivision; any Indian tribe, authorized tribal organization, or Alaska native village; or authorized native organization that has the authority to adopt and enforce floodplain management ordinances for the area under its jurisdiction. In most cases, a community is an incorporated city, town, township, borough, or village, or an unincorporated area of a county or parish. However, some states have statutory authorities that vary from this description.

11. Why is participation in the NFIP on a community basis rather than on an individual basis?

The National Flood Insurance Act of 1968 allows FEMA to make flood insurance available only in those areas where the appropriate public body has adopted adequate floodplain management regulations for its flood-prone areas. Individual citizens cannot regulate building or establish construction priorities for communities. Without community oversight of building activities in the floodplain, the best efforts of some to reduce future flood losses could be undermined or nullified by the careless building of others. Unless the community as a whole is practicing adequate flood hazard mitigation, the potential for loss will not be reduced sufficiently to affect disaster relief costs. Insurance rates also would reflect the probable higher losses that would result without local floodplain management enforcement activities.

12. Is community participation mandatory?

Community participation in the NFIP is voluntary (although some states require NFIP participation as part of their floodplain management program). Each identified flood-prone community must assess its flood hazard and determine whether flood insurance and floodplain management would benefit the community's residents and economy. However, a community that chooses not to participate within 1 year after the flood hazard has been identified and an NFIP map has been provided is subject to the ramifications explained in the answer to Question 20 on page 6.

A community's participation status can significantly affect current and future owners of property located in SFHAs. The decision should be made with full awareness of the consequences of each action.

13. What is the NFIP's Emergency Program?

The Emergency Program is the initial phase of a community's participation in the NFIP and was designed to provide a limited amount of flood insurance. A community participating in the Emergency Program either does not have an identified and mapped flood hazard or has been provided with an FHBM, and the community is required to adopt limited floodplain management standards to control future use of its floodplains. Less than 3 percent of more than 21,000 communities participating in the NFIP remain in the Emergency Program. For additional information on mapping, please refer to the "Flood Hazard Assessment and Mapping Requirements" section of this book, starting on page 27.

14. What is the NFIP's Regular Program?

A community participating in the Regular Program of the NFIP is usually provided with a FIRM and a detailed engineering study, termed a Flood Insurance Study (FIS). (Additional information on FIRMs and FISs is provided in the "Flood Hazard Assessment and Mapping Requirements" section of this book, starting on page 27.) Under the Regular Program, the adoption by the community of more comprehensive floodplain requirements is required for higher amounts of flood insurance.

15. What happens when a participating community chooses not to adopt the effective FIRM and compliant floodplain management ordinance?

As part of their agreement to participate in the NFIP, communities adopt and enforce these ordinances, including FIRMs. If communities do not, they can be placed on probation or suspended from the program. This is done only after FEMA has provided assistance to the community to help it become compliant.

16. What is probation?

Probation is a FEMA-imposed change in a community's status resulting from violations and deficiencies in the administration and enforcement of NFIP local floodplain management regulations.

17. When can a community be placed on probation?

A community can be placed on probation 90 days after FEMA provides written notice to community officials of specific deficiencies. Probation generally is imposed only after FEMA has consulted with the community and has not been able to resolve deficiencies.

18. How long will probation last?

Probation may be continued for up to 1 year after the community corrects all Program deficiencies and remedies all violations to the maximum extent possible.

19. What penalties are imposed when a community is placed on probation?

A surcharge is added to the premium for each policy sold or renewed in the community. The surcharge is effective for at least 1 year after the community's probation period begins. The surcharge is intended to focus the attention of policyholders on the community's noncompliance to help avoid suspension of the community, which has serious adverse impacts on those policyholders. Probation does not affect the availability of flood insurance.

20. What is suspension?

Suspension of a participating community occurs when the community fails to adopt an adequate ordinance, including adopting the most current FIRMs. The community is provided written notice of the impending suspension and granted 30 days in which to show cause why it should not be suspended. Suspension is imposed by FEMA. If suspended, the community becomes non-participating and flood insurance policies cannot be written or renewed. Policies in force at the time of suspension, however, continue in force for the policy term.

FEMA may suspend a participating community when the community fails to enforce its floodplain management regulations for failure to adopt compliant floodplain management measures, or if it repeals or amends previously compliant floodplain management measures. New flood insurance coverage cannot be purchased and policies cannot be renewed in a suspended community. Policies in force at the time of suspension continue in force for the policy term. If the community is suspended following a period of probation, the community is provided written notice of the impending suspension and granted 30 days in which to show cause why it should not be suspended.

21. Is there any way to obtain a community-wide discount on the cost of flood insurance premiums?

All communities in the NFIP adopt and enforce minimum standards for managing construction and development in their Special Flood Hazard Areas. Some communities want to achieve a higher level of safety and protection for their citizens than achieved through implementing minimum standards. When these communities join the NFIP's Community Rating System (CRS), their policyholders may receive a discount on flood insurance premiums. The CRS recognizes communities for their additional efforts to (1) reduce flood damage to insurable property; (2) strengthen and support the insurance aspects of the NFIP; and (3) encourage a comprehensive approach to floodplain management.

Communities that join the CRS receive a rating according to a point system devised to reflect the level of safety provided through the floodplain management activities they implement. CRS communities are assigned a CRS Class, from Class 9 to Class 1, that establishes the level of premium discount policyholders receive. The discount on their annual flood insurance premiums can range from 5% to as much as 45%, based on the community's CRS Class. Policyholders in a CRS Class 9 community receive the lowest discount of 5%. The highest discount of 45% is provided in CRS Class 1 communities and requires the most points. The discount applies to policies for properties located in the Special Flood Hazard Area that qualify. Properties located outside the Special Flood Hazard Area receive smaller discounts.

21a. Why would a community want to join the CRS?

Many communities, especially those with severe flood hazards, high rates of growth, or a history of repeated flooding, are aware of the wide range of actions they can take to reduce flood risk in addition to participating in the NFIP. These actions keep their citizens safer, minimize property damage, build resiliency, and foster a better quality of life within the community. Joining the CRS enables communities to earn insurance premium reductions for their residents for activities already being implemented by a community. Community participation in the CRS provides a national benchmark by which a community can measure its performance in floodplain management. It also provides recognition for a job well done and fosters a sense of community pride.

21b. Why don't all NFIP communities join the CRS?

Some communities believe that participating in the CRS will be time-consuming and require a considerable time investment on their part. It is true that a CRS-participating community must designate a local official to act as the CRS coordinator and point of contact. This person will need to devote some time to become familiar with CRS and complete an application. After the first year, less time is required as the community standardizes its implementation procedures. Certainly, the time commitment for CRS Class 9 or Class 8 communities is much less than that for CRS Class 3, 2, or 1 communities, but the premium discount is also not as great. CRS communities report that the additional commitment is well worth the effort in reduced premiums, a safer community, and increased recognition and awareness of flood risk.

22. How can I find out if my community is in the CRS?

Individuals can phone the general NFIP information number at 1-800-427-4661 to find out if their community participates in the CRS and to learn about the amount of the premium discount.

22a. If my community is not participating in the CRS, what can I do to have my community join?

The decision to join the CRS is a voluntary action of a community's elected officials. As with many community actions, citizens can contact their local elected officials and encourage the community to consider learning more about joining the CRS. Additional technical assistance resources are available through 1-800-427-4661, which can provide further assistance about joining the CRS. The CRS website (http://www.fema.gov/business/nfip/crs.shtm)

also provides additional contact information for technical assistance with applying for the CRS.

23. How can I learn more about the CRS?

The CRS has an informative website, the "CRS Resource Center," at http://www.fema.gov/business/nfip/crs.shtm.

The CRS Resource Center provides introductory materials for the curious as well as technical materials for veteran CRS communities.

24. How can a community acquire the *CRS Coordinator's Manual* and other information describing the program?

The CRS *Coordinator's Manual*, additional CRS publications, and software may be ordered online or by writing, phoning, or faxing a request to the NFIP/CRS. Contact information is listed in the "Additional Resources" section starting on page 52 of this book. All publications are free, and the computer software for completing the application is also available at no charge.

Flood Insurance Information for Prospective Buyers

25. Who may purchase a flood insurance policy?

NFIP coverage is available to all owners of eligible property (a building and/or its contents) located in a community participating in the NFIP. Owners and renters may insure their property against flood loss. Owners of buildings in the course of construction, condominium associations, and owners of residential condominium units in participating communities all may purchase flood insurance.

Condominium associations may purchase insurance coverage on a residential building, including all units, and its commonly owned contents under the Residential Condominium Building Association Policy (RCBAP). The unit owner may separately insure personal contents as well as obtain additional building coverage under the Dwelling Form as long as the unit owner's share of the RCBAP and his/her added coverage do not exceed the statutory limits for a single-family dwelling. The owner of any condominium unit in a non-residential condominium building may purchase only contents coverage for that unit.

26. How can property owners or renters find out if their community participates in the NFIP?

NFIP coverage is available only in participating communities. Almost all of the nation's communities with serious flooding potential have joined the NFIP. The NFIP provides a list of participating communities in the Community Status Book. To learn if your community participates in the NFIP, refer to this list online at http://www.fema.gov/fema/csb.shtm or contact your community official or insurance agent.

27. How can a property owner determine whether or not his or her property is in a Special Flood Hazard Area (SFHA)?

FEMA provides mapped communities with a single paper map of their community. The maps are generally kept in community planning or building permit departments where they should be available for review. In addition, digital flood maps can be viewed on FEMA's Map Information eXchange (FMIX) website at http://msc.fema.gov. Property owners can also contact their insurance agent, who usually has access to FEMA maps or to a Flood Zone Determination service.

28. What types of property may be insured against flood loss?

Insurance may be written on any building eligible for coverage with two or more outside rigid walls and a fully secured roof that is affixed to a permanent site. Buildings must resist flotation, collapse, and lateral movement. The structure must be located in a community that participates in the NFIP.

- Manufactured (i.e., mobile, travel trailers without wheels) homes that are affixed and anchored to a permanent foundation are eligible for coverage.

- Contents coverage for personal belongings located within an eligible building can also be purchased.

29. What kinds of property are not insurable under the NFIP?

Buildings entirely over water or principally below ground, gas and liquid storage tanks, animals, birds, fish, aircraft, wharves, piers, bulkheads, growing crops, shrubbery, land, livestock, roads, machinery or equipment in the open, and most motor vehicles are not insurable through the NFIP.

30. What is a Section 1316 designation and how does it impact flood insurance availability?

A Section 1316 designation is given to buildings that are constructed or altered in such a way as to place them in violation of state or local floodplain management laws, regulations, or ordinances. Contents and personal property contained in these buildings are ineligible for coverage. NFIP flood insurance is not available for buildings with a Section 1316 designation. A community official may request that FEMA rescind the Section 1316 designation when the structure is determined compliant with the floodplain management laws, regulations, or ordinances.

31. How is flood insurance purchased?

After a community joins the NFIP, a policy may be purchased from any licensed property insurance agent or broker who is in good standing in the state in which the agent is licensed or through any agent representing a Write Your Own (WYO) Company, including an employee of the company authorized to issue the coverage. The agent will complete the flood insurance application, obtain the proper supporting documentation required, and determine the rates for establishing the flood insurance premium.

The steps to purchase flood insurance are as follows:

- Identify the flood zone in which the structure is located.

- Complete the flood insurance application.

- If required, obtain supporting documentation (i.e., elevation certificate, photos, zone determination).

- Submit the completed application, supporting documentation, and full premium to the insurer.

32. How are flood insurance premiums calculated?

A number of factors are considered in determining the premium for flood insurance coverage. They include the amount of coverage purchased; the deductible amount selected; the flood zone; location; age of the building; building occupancy; and design of the building (foundation type). For buildings in SFHAs built after the community entered the flood program (Post-FIRM), the elevation of the building in relation to the Base Flood Elevation (BFE) is also a factor in determining the premium.

33. Is the purchase of flood insurance mandatory?

The Flood Disaster Protection Act of 1973 and the National Flood Insurance Reform Act of 1994 mandate that federally regulated, supervised, or insured financial institutions and Federal Agency lenders require flood insurance for buildings located in a participating NFIP community and in an SFHA. Some financial institutions may require flood insurance for properties outside the SFHA as part of their own risk management process.

34. Why is there a requirement to purchase flood insurance in communities that have not suffered flooding in many years, or ever?

A major purpose of the NFIP is to alert communities to the danger of flooding and to assist them in reducing potential property losses from flooding. Historical flood data are only one element used in determining a community's flood risk. More critical determinations can be made by evaluating the community's rainfall and river-flow data, topography, wind velocity, tidal surge, flood-control measures, development (existing and planned), community maps, and other data. Over time, additional development or changes in these factors can alter the flood risk, and flood maps may be revised.

35. Why is my lender requiring the purchase of flood insurance?

Lenders are mandated under the Flood Disaster Protection Act of 1973 and the National Flood Insurance Reform Act of 1994 to require the purchase of flood insurance by property owners who acquire loans from federally regulated, supervised, or insured financial institutions for the acquisition or improvement of land, facilities, or structures located within or to be located within an SFHA.

The lender reviews the current NFIP maps for the community in which the property is located to determine its location relative to the published SFHA and completes the Standard Flood Hazard Determination Form (SFHDF). If the lender determines that the structure is indeed located within the SFHA and the community is participating in the NFIP, the borrower is then notified that flood insurance will be required as a condition of receiving the loan. A similar review and notification are completed whenever a loan is sold on the secondary loan market or perhaps when the lender completes a routine review of its mortgage portfolio.

36. Are lenders required to escrow flood insurance payments?

Yes. If a lender, its servicer, or a Federal Agency lender requires the escrow of taxes, insurance premiums, fees, or any other charges for a loan secured by improved residential real estate or mobile homes, it shall also require the escrow of all premiums and fees for any flood insurance. This requirement applies to loans made, increased, extended, or renewed on or after October 1, 1996.

Requiring lenders to escrow for flood insurance premiums improves compliance with flood insurance requirements by ensuring that homeowners located in Special Flood Hazard Areas obtain and maintain flood insurance for the life of the loan.

37. What if a borrower disagrees with his or her lender's determination that a property is in a flood zone?

If a lending institution is requiring the insurance to meet mandatory flood insurance purchase requirements, the property owners may not contest the requirement if the lending institution has established the requirements as a part of its own standard lending practices. However, if a lending institution is requiring the insurance to meet mandatory flood insurance purchase requirements, the property owner and lender may jointly request that FEMA review the lending institution's determination. This request must be submitted within 45 days of the date the lending institution notified the property owner that a building or manufactured home is in the SFHA and flood insurance is required. In response, FEMA will issue a Letter of Determination Review (LODR). The LODR process should be used as a last resort. Before the LODR process is engaged, the property owners should contact their lender and provide them with additional documentation to support their position.

Some lenders reserve the right in their loan documents to require the purchase of flood insurance regardless of the flood zone. Property owners may not contest the requirement to purchase flood insurance if the lending institution has established the requirement as a part of its own standard lending practice.

38. What is the process and outcome of the LODR on the lender's determination?

The LODR does not result in an amendment or revision to the NFIP map. It only upholds or overturns the lender's determination. The LODR remains in effect until the NFIP map panel affecting the subject building or manufactured home is revised. The LODR process does not consider the elevation of the structure above the flood level. It considers only the location of the structure relative to the SFHA shown on the effective FIRM. FEMA confirms the location of the structure on the FIRM by examining the data source used by the lender to make the determination.

A fee must be submitted with all LODR requests. The fee payment may be in the form of a check or money order, in U.S. dollars, made payable to the "National Flood Insurance Program."

39. How many buildings or locations (and their contents) may be insured on each policy?

Only one building and its contents can be insured on a policy. However, the Dwelling Form of the Standard Flood Insurance Policy (SFIP) does provide coverage for up to 10 percent of the policy amount for appurtenant detached garages.

40. What is the flood insurance policy term?

Flood insurance coverage is available for a 1-year term.

41. Is there a minimum coverage requirement for a flood insurance policy?

No, there is no minimum coverage requirement if coverage is being purchased voluntarily.

However, if coverage is being purchased as the result of a lender requirement (mandatory purchase requirement), the amount of flood insurance required must be at least equal to the lesser of (1) the outstanding principal balance of the loan, (2) the maximum amount available under the NFIP, or (3) the total insurable value of the property.

Some lenders reserve the right in their loan documents to require the purchase of flood insurance above the amount required by law. If so, they may require the amount of coverage to be as high as the building's replacement cost value.

Property owners should consult with their insurance agent and lender to determine the appropriate amount of insurance to purchase. This does not apply to the Group Flood Insurance Policy (GFIP).

42. Can an NFIP policy be rated based on the FIRM that was in effect when the building was constructed, even if a FIRM is revised?

Yes. To recognize policyholders who built in compliance with the FIRM that was effective when the building was constructed, the NFIP has "grandfather rules" that allow policies to be rated based on the FIRM that was in effect when the structure was built. Supporting documentation that confirms the flood zone and/or BFE information from the prior FIRM is required to grandfather the rating. NFIP "grandfather rules" do not apply to the low-cost Preferred Risk Policy (PRP). The FIRM in effect when the PRP is effective determines eligibility for the PRP.

43. If a building is substantially improved or damaged, can the rating be grandfathered to a prior FIRM that was in effect when the building was originally constructed?

No. If a building is substantially improved or damaged, the FIRM in effect at the time of improvement or damage must be used for rating.

44. When a property's flood zone changes from a non–Special Flood Hazard Zone (SFHA) to an SFHA as a result of a FIRM update, can the property continue to be rated using the PRP?

Yes. Because flood zone revisions on updated FIRMs have resulted in a financial challenge for many homeowners, FEMA has implemented a measure that provides financial relief by delaying the applicability of the SFHA standard rating for 2 years. Buildings newly mapped into an SFHA by a map effective on or after October 1, 2008, are eligible for the PRP for 2 years beginning on January 1, 2011, or the map change effective date, whichever is later. The building must also meet the PRP loss history requirements. At the end of the extended PRP eligibility period, the policy would be renewed as a standard-rated policy, and may be eligible for grandfathering on a standard-rated policy.

45. Are there grandfather rules to allow policyholders to maintain the current rating despite a map revision that places property in a higher-rated flood zone?

Yes. To recognize policyholders who have built in compliance with the FIRM and/or remained loyal customers of the NFIP by maintaining continuous coverage, FEMA has "grandfather rules." These rules allow such policyholders to benefit in the rating for that building. For such buildings, the insured would have the option of using the current rating criteria for that building or having the premium rate determined by using the BFE and/or flood zone on a previous FIRM that was in effect when the building was originally constructed (for those built in compliance) or when coverage was first obtained (for those with continuous coverage). This leads to cost savings to insureds when the new map resulting from a map revision would result in a higher premium rate.

46. Is there a waiting period for flood insurance to become effective?

Yes. There is a 30-day waiting period before flood coverage goes into effect. The effective date of a new policy will be

- 12:01 a.m., local time, on the 30th calendar day after the application date and the presentment of premium.

However, there are exceptions in which the 30-day waiting period does not apply:

- In connection with making, increasing, extending, or renewing a loan, whether conventional or otherwise, flood insurance that is initially purchased in connection with the making, increasing, extending, or renewal of a loan shall be effective at the time of loan closing, provided that the policy is applied for and the presentment of premium is made at the time of or prior to the loan closing.

- In connection with lender requirement, the 30-day waiting period does not apply when flood insurance is required as a result of a lender determining that a loan on a building in an SFHA that does not have flood insurance coverage should be protected by flood insurance. The coverage is effective upon the completion of an application and the presentment of payment of premium.

- When the initial purchase of flood insurance is in connection with the revision or updating of a Flood Hazard Boundary Map (FHBM) or Flood Insurance Rate Map (FIRM): During the 13-month period beginning on the effective date of the map revision, the effective date of a new policy shall be 12:01 a.m., local time, following the day after the application date and the presentment of premium. This rule applies only where the FHBM or FIRM is revised to show the building to be in an SFHA when it had not been in an SFHA.

47. What is "presentment of payment"?

Presentment of premium is defined as:

- The date of the check or credit card payment by the applicant or the applicant's representative if the premium payment is not part of a loan closing.

- The date of the closing, if the premium payment is part of a loan closing.

For a loan closing, premium payment from the escrow account (lender's check), title company, or settlement attorney is considered made at closing, regardless of when the check is received by the writing company.

48. Is there a special rating procedure applicable to coastal high hazard areas (V Zones)?

In calculating the applicable rates for buildings that were constructed or substantially improved in V Zones after October 1, 1981, the actuarial formula takes into account the ability of the building to withstand the impact of wave action. The agent must follow the special instructions in the NFIP *Flood Insurance Manual* in preparing an application for coverage for buildings located in V Zones. (See the "Flood Hazard Assessment and Mapping Requirements" section starting on page 27 for a further explanation of V Zones.)

49. What is the Coastal Barrier Resources System (CBRS)?

The Coastal Barrier Resources Act (CBRA) of 1982 established the John H. Chafee Coastal Barrier Resources System (CBRS), a defined set of coastal barrier units located along the Atlantic, Gulf of Mexico, Great Lakes, Puerto Rico, and U.S. Virgin Islands coasts. These areas are delineated on a set of maps that are enacted into law by Congress and maintained by the Department of the Interior through the U.S. Fish and Wildlife Service. Most new Federal expenditures and financial assistance are prohibited within the CBRS. The prohibition that is most significant to homeowners and insurance agents is the denial of Federal flood insurance through the NFIP for new or substantially improved structures within the CBRS. The CBRA does not prevent development and it imposes no restrictions on development conducted with non-Federal funds. Congress enacted the CBRA to minimize the loss of human life, wasteful Federal expenditures, and the damage to natural resources associated with coastal barriers.

What are the differences between System Units and Otherwise Protected Areas (OPAs)? The CBRS contains two types of units: System Units and Otherwise Protected Areas (OPAs). System Units are generally comprised of private lands that were relatively undeveloped at the time of their designation with the CBRS. The boundaries of these units are generally intended to follow geomorphic, development, or cultural features. Most new Federal expenditures and financial assistance, including Federal flood insurance, are prohibited within System Units. OPAs are generally comprised of lands held by a qualified organization primarily for wildlife refuge, sanctuary, recreational, or natural resource conservation purposes. The boundaries of these units are generally intended to coincide with the boundaries of conservation or recreation areas such as state parks and national wildlife refuges. The only Federal spending prohibition within OPAs is the prohibition on Federal flood insurance.

50. Is Federal flood insurance available in the CBRS?

Federal flood insurance is available in a CBRS area if the subject building was constructed (or permitted and under construction) before the CBRS unit's prohibition date. CBRS areas designated by the 1982 Act prohibit the sale of Federal flood insurance for structures built or substantially improved after October 1, 1983. For subsequent additions to the CBRS, the insurance prohibition date is shown on the FIRM. Flood insurance may be obtained for structures located in OPAs with written documentation from the government body overseeing the area certifying that the structure is used in a manner consistent with the purpose for which the area is protected. If an existing insured structure is substantially improved or damaged, any Federal flood insurance policy will not be renewed. If a Federal flood insurance policy is issued in error, it will be canceled and the premium refunded; no claim can be paid, even if the error is not found until a claim is made.

51. Can flood insurance be canceled at the request of the insured with a refund of premium?

Yes, in some cases. For example, if the policyholder sold the property and no longer has an insurable interest in it, the policy can be canceled with a pro-rated return.

However, due to the seasonal nature of flooding, and to protect the lender's interest, there are limited valid cancellations reasons. The valid cancellation reasons and the proper procedures and documentation required to cancel a policy are outlined in the NFIP *Flood Insurance Manual*.

To request a cancellation, the policyholder should contact the insurance agent servicing the policy.

52. Is there a "grace period" for renewing an NFIP policy after expiration?

All policies expire at 12:01 a.m. on the last day of the policy term.

However, coverage remains in force for 30 days after the expiration of the policy, and claims for losses that occur during the period will be honored provided that the full renewal premium is received within 30 days of the policy expiration date.

Coverage also remains in force for the benefit of any mortgagee, but only for 30 days after the mortgagee is notified of the cancellation or expiration.

53. What is the requirement for purchasing flood insurance after receiving disaster assistance?

The National Flood Insurance Reform Act of 1994 requires individuals in SFHAs who receive disaster assistance after September 23, 1994, for flood disaster losses to real or personal property to purchase and maintain flood insurance coverage for as long as they live in the dwelling.

Coverage

54. How much flood insurance coverage is available?

The following coverage limits are available under the Dwelling Form and the General Property Form of the Standard Flood Insurance Policy (SFIP). Coverage limits under the Residential Condominium Building Association Policy (RCBAP) are listed in the NFIP *Flood Insurance Manual*.

	Emergency Program	Regular Program
Building Coverage		
Single-family dwelling	$ 35,000*	$250,000
Two- to four-family dwelling	$ 35,000*	$250,000
Other residential	$100,000*	$250,000
Non-residential	$100,000*	$500,000
Contents Coverage		
Residential	$ 10,000	$100,000
Non-residential	$100,000	$500,000

* Under the Emergency Program, higher limits of building coverage are available in Alaska, Hawaii, the U.S. Virgin Islands, and Guam.

55. Are there limitations on the amount of insurance available for certain types of property?

General coverage limitations are explained in the answers to Questions 28 and 29. In addition, items such as artwork, photographs, collectibles, memorabilia, rare books, autographed items, jewelry, watches, gems, furs, and articles of gold, silver, or platinum are limited to $2,500 coverage in the aggregate. This limitation does not apply to other items that are personal property or household contents usual or incidental to the occupancy of the building as a residence.

In addition, there are coverage limitations for items located in basements, or in an enclosed area under an elevated floor, for Post-FIRM structures located in an SFHA.

The *General Property Form* limits the recoverable amount for Pollution Damage to $10,000. Refer to the *General Property Form* under Section III. Property Covered, Part C. Coverage C—Other Coverages for other limitations that apply for this coverage. For other limitations under the SFIP, see the current policy or contact a property insurance agent or broker.

56. What flood losses are covered?

Direct physical losses "by flood," losses resulting from flood-related erosion caused by waves or currents of water activity exceeding anticipated cyclical levels, or caused by a severe storm, flash flood, abnormal tidal surge, which result in flooding, as defined in the SFIP. Damage caused by mudflows, as specifically defined in the policy forms, is covered.

57. What coverage is available in basements and in enclosed areas beneath the lowest elevated floor of an elevated building located in an SFHA built after the community entered the NFIP (Post-FIRM)?

Coverage is provided for foundation elements, including posts, pilings, piers, or other support systems for elevated buildings. Coverage also is available for basement and enclosure utility connections, as well as for certain mechanical equipment necessary for the habitability of a building, such as furnaces, water heaters, clothes washers and dryers, food freezers and the food in them, air conditioners, heat pumps, electrical junctions, and circuit breaker boxes. Finished structural elements such as paneling and linoleum, and contents items such as rugs and furniture are not covered. The SFIP has a complete list of covered elements and equipment.

For a complete list of coverage, refer to any of the SFIP forms, Section III. Property Covered, Part A. Building Property – 8. a. (1) through (17) and b., for building items covered. For Personal Property, refer to Section III. Property Covered, Part B. Personal Property – 4. a., b., and c.

58. What is a basement?

The NFIP's definition of "basement" includes any part of a building where all sides of the floor are located below ground level. Even though a room may have windows and constitute living quarters, it is still considered to be a basement if the floor is below ground level on all sides.

59. Are losses from land subsidence, sewer backup, or seepage of water covered?

The NFIP will pay for losses from land subsidence under certain circumstances. Subsidence of land along a lakeshore or similar body of water that results from the erosion or undermining of the shoreline caused by waves or currents of water exceeding cyclical levels that result in a flood is covered. All other land subsidence is excluded.

Unless there is a general condition of flooding in the area and the flood is the proximate cause of sewer or drain backup, sump pump discharge or overflow, or seepage of water, the NFIP does not insure for direct physical loss caused directly or indirectly by any of the following:

- Backups through sewers or drains;
- Discharges or overflows from a sump, a sump pump, or related equipment; or
- Seepage or leaks on or through the covered property.

60. Does the NFIP apply a deductible to losses?

A minimum deductible is applied separately to a building and its contents, although both may be damaged in the same flood. Optional deductibles are available, and an insurance agent can provide information on specific amounts of available deductibles. Optional high deductibles reduce policy premiums but will have to be approved by the mortgage lender.

When a building is under construction, alteration, or repair and does not have at least two rigid exterior walls and a fully secured roof at the time of the loss, the deductible amount will be two times the deductible that would otherwise apply to a completed building. The deductible does not apply to:

- Loss avoidance measures;
- Condominium loss assessments; or
- Increased cost of compliance.

61. Are costs of preventive measures covered under the SFIP?

Some are. When an insured building is in imminent danger of being flooded, the reasonable expenses incurred by the insured for the removal of insured property to a safe location and return will be reimbursed up to $1,000, and the purchase of sandbags and sand to fill them, plastic sheeting and lumber used in connection with them, pumps, fill for temporary levees, and wood will be reimbursed up to $1,000. No deductible is applied to this coverage.

Note: The coverage for Sandbags, Supplies, and Labor applies only if damage to insured property by or from flood is imminent, and the threat of flood damage is apparent enough to lead a person of common prudence to anticipate flood damage.

One of the following must also occur:

(a) A general and temporary condition of flooding in the area near the described location must occur, even if the flood does not reach the insured building; or

(b) A legally authorized official must issue an evacuation order or other civil order for the community in which the insured building is located calling for measures to preserve life and property from the peril of flood. This coverage does not increase the Coverage A or Coverage B limit of liability.

For additional information, refer to any of the SFIP forms, Section III. Property Covered, Part C. Coverage C – Other Coverages: 2. a. and b.

62. Does insurance under the NFIP provide coverage at replacement cost?

Replacement cost coverage is available for a single-family dwelling, insured under the Dwelling Form that is the policyholder's principal residence and is insured for at least 80 percent of the building's total insurable value at the time of the loss, or the maximum amount of insurance available under the Program. Replacement cost coverage does not apply to manufactured (i.e., mobile) homes smaller than certain dimensions specified in the policy.

Losses are adjusted on a replacement cost basis for residential condominium buildings insured under the Residential Condominium Building Association Policy (RCBAP). However, coverage amounts less than 80 percent of the building's full replacement cost value (RCV) at the time of loss will be subject to a coinsurance penalty.

Building losses under the General Property Form are always adjusted on an actual cash value basis.

Contents losses are always adjusted on an actual cash value basis. Actual cash value means the replacement cost of an insured item of property at the time of loss, less the value of physical depreciation of the item damaged.

63. Does the Standard Flood Insurance Policy (SFIP) provide additional living expenses if the insured dwelling is flood damaged and cannot be occupied while repairs are being made?

No. The policy covers only direct physical flood damage to the dwelling and does not provide for additional living expenses.

64. What is Increased Cost of Compliance (ICC) coverage?

Increased Cost of Compliance (ICC) coverage under the SFIP provides for the payment of a claim to help pay for the cost to comply with state or community floodplain management laws or ordinances from a flood event in which a building has been declared substantially damaged or repetitively damaged. When an insured building is damaged by a flood and the state or community declares the building to be substantially damaged or repetitively damaged, ICC coverage will help pay for the cost to elevate, floodproof, demolish, or relocate the building up to a maximum benefit of $30,000. This coverage is in addition to the building coverage for the repair of actual physical damages from flood under the SFIP.

65. Is there a limit to the amount a policyholder can collect under ICC coverage?

Yes. The maximum amount a policyholder may collect under ICC is $30,000. This amount is in addition to the amount the policyholder receives for physical damages by flood. The total amount the policyholder receives for combined physical structural damage from flood and ICC is always capped by the maximum limit of coverage established by Congress. The maximum amount collectible for both ICC and physical damage from flood for a single-family dwelling is $250,000.

66. Is ICC premium included in all Standard Flood Insurance Policies?

Yes—however, not all buildings are eligible for ICC coverage. To be eligible for ICC coverage, a building must be declared substantially damaged, and there must be mitigation activities to reduce the building's exposure to future flood damage. Refer to Section D of the policy form for more information regarding ICC coverage.

Filing a Flood Insurance Claim

67. How does a policyholder file a claim for flood loss?

A flood insurance policyholder should immediately report any flood loss to the insurance company or agent who wrote the policy. A claims adjuster will be assigned the loss, and the policyholder must file a "proof of loss" within 60 days of the date of loss. A policyholder whose policy is with a WYO Company must follow the company's claim procedures. The 60-day time limit for filling a proof of loss remains the same.

68. What is a "proof of loss"?

A proof of loss—the policyholder's valuation of claimed damages—is a sworn statement made by the policyholder that substantiates the insurance claim and is required to be submitted to the NFIP or WYO Company within 60 days of the loss. A printed form usually is available from the adjuster assigned to the claim.

Note: Some WYO Companies and the NFIP Direct Servicing Agent may require the proof of loss to be affirmed by a public notary.

69. What is a "loss in progress"?

A loss in progress occurs when actual flood damage to a building or its contents started before the inception of the policy, or when coverage is added at the insured's request when a flood is imminent.

70. Is a loss in progress covered?

The NFIP does not cover damage caused by a loss in progress under any of the flood insurance policies.

71. What is the maximum that can be collected for a loss under the NFIP policy?

An insured will never be paid more than the value of the covered loss, less deductible, up to the amounts of insurance purchased. Therefore, purchasing insurance to value is an important consideration. The amount of insurance a property owner needs should be discussed with an insurance agent or broker.

Floodplain Management Requirements

72. What is the role of the community in floodplain management?

When a community chooses to join the NFIP, it must adopt and enforce minimum floodplain management standards for participation. FEMA works closely with state and local officials to identify flood hazard areas and flood risks. The floodplain management requirements within the Special Flood Hazard Area (SFHA) are designed to prevent new development from increasing the flood threat and to protect new and existing buildings from anticipated flood events.

When a community chooses to join the NFIP, it must require permits for all development in the SFHA and ensure that construction materials and methods used will minimize future flood damage. Permit files must contain documentation to substantiate how buildings were actually constructed. In return, the Federal Government makes flood insurance available for eligible buildings and their contents within the community.

Communities must ensure that their adopted floodplain management ordinance and enforcement procedures meet program requirements. Local regulations must be updated when additional data are provided by FEMA or when Federal or state standards are revised.

73. Do state governments assist in implementing the NFIP?

At the request of FEMA, each governor has designated an agency of state or territorial government to coordinate that state's or territory's NFIP activities. These agencies often assist communities in developing and adopting necessary floodplain management measures through a grant from FEMA through the Community Assistance Program, State Support Services Element (CAP-SSSE).

Some states require more stringent measures than those of the NFIP. For contact information, see the list of "State NFIP Coordinating Agencies" starting on page 47 of this book.

74. Do Federal requirements take precedence over state requirements?

The regulatory requirements set forth by FEMA are the minimum measures acceptable for NFIP participation. More stringent requirements adopted by the local community or state take precedence over the minimum regulatory requirements established for flood insurance availability.

FEMA supports state-initiated enforcement actions of higher standards by providing technical assistance and initiating FEMA enforcement actions where appropriate, as defined in 44 CFR §59.24. If a state chooses not to enforce its own regulations, FEMA shall limit its enforcement actions to compliance with NFIP criteria; or, after all technical assistance has been exhausted, FEMA may strongly suggest that the provision be omitted from state law until adequate progress can be shown that the provision is being fully enforced.

75. What is meant by "floodplain management measures"?

"Floodplain management measures" refers to an overall community program of corrective and preventive measures for reducing future flood damage. These measures take a variety of forms and generally include zoning, subdivision, or building requirements, and special-purpose floodplain ordinances.

76. Do the floodplain management measures required by the NFIP affect existing buildings?

The minimum Federal requirements affect an existing building only when it is substantially damaged or improved. There may also be situations where a building has been constructed in accordance with a local floodplain management ordinance, and the owner subsequently alters it in violation of the local building code, without a permit. Such unapproved modifications to an existing building may not meet the minimum Federal requirements.

A floodplain management ordinance should define "existing construction" as, for the purposes of determining flood insurance rates, structures for which the "start of construction" commenced before the effective date of the FIRM or before January 1, 1975, for FIRMs effective before that date.

77. What constitutes "substantial improvement" or "substantial damage"?

"Substantial improvement" means any rehabilitation, addition, or other improvement of a building when the cost of the improvement equals or exceeds 50 percent of the market value of the building before start of construction of the improvement. The term includes buildings that have incurred "substantial damage," which means damage of any origin sustained by a building when the cost of restoring the building to its pre-damaged condition would equal or exceed 50 percent of the market value of the building before the damage occurred. Substantial damage is determined regardless of the actual repair work performed.

Substantial improvement or damage does not, however, include any project for improvement of a building to correct existing violations of state or local health, sanitary, or safety code specifications identified by local code enforcement officials as the minimum specifications necessary to ensure safe living conditions. Also excluded from the substantial improvement requirement are alterations to historic buildings as defined by the NFIP.

78. Do the floodplain management requirements apply to construction taking place outside the SFHAs within a community?

The local floodplain management regulations required by the NFIP apply only in SFHAs. However, communities may regulate development in areas of moderate flood hazard.

79. Can modifications be made to the basic floodplain management requirement?

In developing their floodplain management ordinances, participating communities must meet at least the minimum regulatory standards issued by FEMA. NFIP standards and policies are reviewed periodically and revised whenever appropriate.

If communities are having difficulty developing an ordinance that is compliant with the minimum regulatory standards, they should contact their state NFIP Coordinator and appropriate FEMA Regional Office.

80. Does elevating a structure on posts or pilings remove a building from the SFHA?

Elevating a structure on posts or pilings does not remove a building from the SFHA. If the ground around the supporting posts or pilings is within the floodplain, the building is still at risk. Ground saturation can lead to decreased load-bearing capacity of the soil supporting the posts or pilings, which can lead to partial or full collapse of the structure. Flood insurance will be required as a condition of receipt of Federal or federally regulated financing for the structure. FEMA recommends securely elevating structures above the SFHA to reduce the risk to life and property, and has established a rating structure that could result in significant savings in premium costs for those who elevate.

81. Where can additional information on floodplain management requirements of the NFIP be found?

Interested parties can find additional information on floodplain management requirements of the NFIP by visiting the website http://www.fema.gov/plan/prevent/floodplain/index.shtm.

Flood Hazard Assessment and Mapping Requirements

82. What is the Flood Insurance Study (FIS) process?

To determine what the flood hazards are for an area, FEMA performs an engineering study called a Flood Insurance Study (FIS). An FIS studies shallow flood areas and flood hazard areas along rivers, streams, coasts, and lakes.

An FIS is based on different information, including:

- Historic information (such as river flow, storm tide, and rainfall data);
- Meteorologic data;
- Topographic data;
- Hydrologic data;
- Hydraulic data;
- Open-space conditions;
- Flood-control works; *and*
- Development.

The results of the FIS are shown on FEMA's flood maps called Flood Insurance Rate Maps, or FIRMs, and in the accompanying description of the study called an FIS report. FIRMs and FIS reports are available through the Map Service Center.

83. How are communities involved in the Flood Insurance Study process?

Prior to engaging community officials, FEMA coordinates with other Federal agencies (e.g., U.S. Corps of Engineers) to identify and gather existing data that may inform FIS development. FEMA then holds Discovery Meetings with community officials and other interested parties to review the data and obtain all additional relevant information to ensure that the FIS is as valuable and accurate as possible. Following the Discovery Meeting, FEMA determines where FIS projects will proceed.

FEMA continues to engage communities throughout FIS process with:

- Resilience Meetings, where flood risk awareness and mitigation planning are discussed;
- An optional Flood Study Review Meeting, where draft flood risk products are presented to community officials; *and*

- A Consultation Coordination Officer (CCO) Meeting/Open House where the preliminary FIRM, FIS, and related flood risk products are shared with community officials and citizens.

Communities are given the opportunity to review the preliminary maps and provide comments and appeals on the engineering and mapping that went into the map. Once maps are finalized, communities must adopt the final map to stay in good standing with the NFIP.

84. What is the difference between a Flood Hazard Boundary Map (FHBM) and a Flood Insurance Rate Map (FIRM)?

A Flood Hazard Boundary Map (FHBM) is based on approximate data and identifies the SFHAs within a community. It is used in the NFIP's Emergency Program for floodplain management and insurance purposes. A FIRM or Digital Flood Insurance Rate Map (DFIRM) is normally issued following a flood risk assessment conducted in connection with a community's conversion to the NFIP's Regular Program. If a detailed assessment, termed a Flood Insurance Study (FIS) (see the answer to Question 82 for an explanation of the FIS process), has been performed, the FIRM will show Base Flood Elevations (BFEs) and insurance risk zones in addition to floodplain boundaries. The FIRM may also show a delineation of the regulatory floodway. (See the answer to Question 88 for a description of "regulatory floodway.") After the effective date of the FIRM, the community's floodplain management ordinance must be in compliance with appropriate Regular Program requirements. Actuarial rates, based on the risk zone designations shown on the FIRM, are then applied for newly constructed, substantially improved, and substantially damaged buildings.

85. How are flood hazard areas and flood levels determined?

Flood hazard areas are determined using statistical analyses of records of riverflow, storm tides, erosion, wave heights, and rainfall; information obtained through consultation with the community; floodplain topographic surveys; and coastal, hydrologic, and hydraulic analyses. The FIS covers those areas subject to flooding from rivers and streams, along coastal areas and lakeshores, and/or shallow flooding areas.

86. What is the role of the local community in its flood hazard assessment?

Community officials, FEMA representatives, and the selected contractor meet to discuss the areas to be studied and the level of study required prior to the study. FEMA works closely with community officials and the contractors before and during the study to obtain all relevant information and to obtain community input before the FIRM and collateral FIS report are published. Additionally, these parties meet to discuss technical and administrative procedures and ensure accurate study results. Community officials also hold public meetings to explain the assessment process to the public.

87. What flood hazard zones are shown on the FIRM and what do they mean?

Several areas of flood hazard are commonly identified on the DFIRM and FIRM. One of these areas is the SFHA, which is defined as the area that would be inundated by the flood event having a 1 percent chance of being equaled or exceeded in any given year. The 1-percent-annual-chance flood is also referred to as the "base flood." SFHAs are labeled as Zone A, Zone AO, Zone AH, Zones A1–A30, Zone AE, Zone 99, Zone AR, Zone AR/AE, Zone AR/AH, Zone AR/AO, Zone AR/A1–A30, Zone AR/A, Zone V, Zone VE, and Zones V1–V30. Moderate flood hazard areas, labeled Zone B, are also shown on the FIRM or DFIRM and are the areas between the limits of the base flood and the 0.2-percent-annual-chance flood. The areas of minimal flood hazard, which are the areas outside the SFHA and higher than the elevation of the 0.2-percent-annual-chance flood, are labeled Zone C. On new and revised maps, Zone X is used in place of Zones B and C. An unshaded Zone X holds the same meaning as the labeled Zone B. A shaded Zone X can mean any of the following: the area is in the 0.2 floodplain; is protected by a levee; is subject to inundation by a flood event having a 1 percent chance of reaching less than a 1.0-foot depth; is subject to inundation by a 1-percent-annual-chance flood within an area of less than 1 square mile; or is subject to inundation by a 1-percent-annual-chance flood determined using future conditions. The definitions for the various flood hazard areas are below.

Zone V: Primary frontal dunes and areas along coasts subject to inundation by the 1-percent-annual-chance flood event with additional hazards associated with storm-induced waves. Because detailed coastal analyses have not been performed, no BFEs or flood depths are shown. Mandatory flood insurance purchase requirements apply.

Zones VE and V1–V30: Primary frontal dunes and areas along coasts subject to inundation by the 1-percent-annual-chance flood event with additional hazards due to storm-induced velocity wave action. BFEs derived from detailed hydraulic coastal analyses are shown within these zones. Mandatory flood insurance purchase requirements apply. Zone VE is used on new and revised maps in place of Zones V1–V30.

Zone A: Areas subject to inundation by the 1-percent-annual-chance flood event. Because detailed hydraulic analyses have not been performed, no BFEs or flood depths are shown. Mandatory flood insurance purchase requirements apply.

Zones AE and A1–A30: Areas subject to inundation by the 1-percent-annual-chance flood event determined by detailed methods. BFEs are shown within these zones. Mandatory flood insurance purchase requirements apply. (Zone AE is used on new and revised maps in place of Zones A1–A30.)

Zone AH: Areas subject to inundation by 1-percent-annual-chance shallow flooding (usually areas of ponding) where average depths are 1–3 feet. BFEs derived from detailed hydraulic analyses are shown in this zone. Mandatory flood insurance purchase requirements apply.

Zone AO: Areas subject to inundation by 1-percent-annual-chance shallow flooding (usually sheet flow on sloping terrain) where average depths are 1–3 feet. Average flood depths derived from detailed hydraulic analyses are shown within this zone. Mandatory flood insurance purchase requirements apply.

Zone A99: Areas subject to inundation by the 1-percent-annual-chance flood event, but which will ultimately be protected upon completion of an under-construction Federal flood protection system. These are areas of special flood hazard where enough progress has been made on the construction of a protection system, such as dikes, dams, and levees, to consider it complete for insurance rating purposes. Zone A99 may be used only when the flood protection system has reached specified statutory progress toward completion. No BFEs or flood depths are shown. Mandatory flood insurance purchase requirements apply.

Zone AR: Areas that result from the decertification of a previously accredited flood protection system that is determined to be in the process of being restored to provide base flood protection. Mandatory flood insurance purchase requirements apply.

Zones AR/AE, AR/AH, AR/AO, AR/A1–A30, and AR/A: Dual flood zones that, because of the risk of flooding from other water sources that the flood protection system does not contain, will continue to be subject to flooding after the flood protection system is adequately restored. Mandatory flood insurance purchase requirements apply.

Zones B, C, and X: Areas identified in a community's FIS as areas of moderate or minimal hazard from the principal source of flood in the area. However, buildings in these zones could be flooded by severe, concentrated rainfall coupled with inadequate local drainage systems. Local stormwater drainage systems are not normally considered in a community's FIS. The failure of a local drainage system creates areas of high flood risk within these rate zones. Flood insurance is available in participating communities but is not required by regulation in these zones. Zone X is used on new and revised maps in place of Zones B and C.

Zone D: Unstudied areas where flood hazards are undetermined, but flooding is possible. No mandatory flood insurance purchase requirements apply, but coverage is available in participating communities.

88. What is a regulatory floodway, and who designates it?

A regulatory floodway, which is adopted into a community's floodplain management ordinance, includes the stream channel plus the portion of the floodplain outside of the channel banks. That portion must be kept free from encroachment so that water flows may pass without increasing flood levels by more than 1.0 foot (some states specify a smaller allowable increase). The intention of the floodway designation is not to preclude development. Rather, it is intended to assist communities in managing floodplain development and its impacts on other property owners. The community is responsible for prohibiting encroachments including fill, new construction, and substantial improvements within the floodway unless hydrologic and hydraulic analyses show it will not increase flood levels within the community. In areas that fall within the 1-percent-annual-chance floodplain, but are outside the floodway (termed the "floodway fringe"), development must cause no more than a 1.0-foot increase in the 1-percent-annual-chance flood levels.

89. What procedures are available for changing or correcting a FIRM?

FEMA has established administrative procedures for changing effective FIRMs, DFIRMs, and FIS reports based on new or revised scientific or technical data. A physical change to the affected DFIRM and FIRM panels, and portions of the FIS report, are referenced as a Physical Map Revision (PMR). Changes can also be made by a Letter of Map Change (LOMC). The three LOMC categories are Letter of Map Amendment (LOMA), Letter of Map Revision Based on Fill (LOMR-F), and Letter of Map Revision (LOMR). They are discussed in more detail in Questions 92–94.

90. What is a Physical Map Revision (PMR)?

A PMR is an official republication of a community's NFIP map to make changes to Base Flood Elevations (BFEs), floodplain boundary delineations, regulatory floodways, and planimetric features. These changes typically occur as a result of structural works or improvements, annexations resulting in additional flood hazard areas, or correction to BFEs or SFHAs.

A PMR can be initiated by FEMA to restudy an area that covers multiple map panels, but does not cover an entire community or county. A PMR can also be initiated when an application for an LOMR from the community is received by FEMA, but the revised area is greater than one panel. In that case, FEMA processes the map change as a PMR rather than an LOMR.

A community's chief executive officer must submit scientific and technical data to FEMA to support the request for a PMR. The data will be analyzed, and the map will be revised if warranted. The community is provided with copies of the revised information and is afforded a review period. When BFEs are changed, a 90-day appeal period is provided. A 6-month period for formal approval of the revised map(s) is also provided.

91. What is a Letter of Map Revision Based on Fill (LOMR-F)?

An LOMR-F is a letter that officially revises an effective FEMA map. An LOMR-F states FEMA's determination as to whether a structure or parcel has been elevated on fill above the BFE and is, therefore, excluded from the SFHA.

92. What is a Letter of Map Amendment (LOMA)?

A LOMA is a letter that officially revises an effective FEMA NFIP map. A LOMA results from an administrative procedure involving the review of scientific or technical data submitted by the owner or lessee of property who believes the property has incorrectly been included in a designated SFHA or has been incorrectly identified in the wrong SFHA. A LOMA amends the currently effective FEMA map and establishes that a specific property is not located in the SFHA or is located within the correct SFHA.

93. What is a Letter of Map Revision (LOMR)?

An LOMR is a letter that officially revises the currently effective FEMA map. It is used to change flood zones, floodplain and floodway delineations, flood elevations, and planimetric features. All requests for LOMRs should be made to FEMA through the chief executive officer of the community, since it is the community that must adopt any changes and revisions to the map. If the request for an LOMR is not submitted through the chief executive officer of the community, evidence must be submitted that the community has been notified of the request.

94. What is a Conditional Letter of Map Revision (CLOMR)?

A Conditional Letter of Map Revision (CLOMR) is FEMA's formal review and comment on whether a proposed project complies with the minimum NFIP floodplain management criteria. NFIP maps are based on existing, rather than proposed, conditions. Because flood insurance is a financial protection mechanism from hazards for property owners and lending institutions, flood insurance ratings must be made accordingly. Communities, developers, and property owners often undertake projects that may alter or mitigate flood hazards and would like FEMA's comment before constructing them. A CLOMR contains formal review and comment. If a proposed project complies with the minimum NFIP floodplain management criteria, the CLOMR also describes any eventual revisions that will be made to the NFIP maps upon completion of the project.

While obtaining a CLOMR may be desired, obtaining conditional approval is not automatically required by NFIP regulations for all projects in the floodway or 1-percent-annual-chance floodplain. A CLOMR is required only for those projects that will result in a 1-percent-annual-chance water surface elevation increase of greater than 1.0 foot for streams with BFEs specified, but no floodway designated, or any 1-percent-annual-chance water surface elevation increase for proposed construction within a regulatory floodway. The technical data needed to support a CLOMR request generally involve detailed hydrologic and hydraulic analyses and are very similar to the data needed for an LOMR request.

In addition to the situations described above, property owners and developers who intend to place structures in the 1-percent-annual-chance floodplain may need to demonstrate to the lending institutions and local officials before construction that proposed structures will be above the Base Flood Elevation. If the project involves only the elevation of structures on natural high ground, they can request a Conditional Letter of Map Amendment (CLOMA) from FEMA. If the elevation of structures on earthen fill is the sole component of the project and there is no fill placed in the regulatory floodway, they can request from FEMA a CLOMR based on fill (CLOMR-F). All LOMC requests, including CLOMAs, CLOMRs, and CLOMR-Fs, should be sent to the LOMC Clearinghouse. The address of the Clearinghouse can be found on page 42 and in the map revision application forms. Until a property shown in an SFHA on the latest version of the FIRM is formally removed from that SFHA via a LOMA, LOMR-F, or LOMR, it remains in the SFHA and is subject to the community floodplain management ordinance and the mandatory flood insurance purchase requirement.

95. Who in FEMA should be contacted to initiate a LOMA, LOMR, or Physical Map Revision (PMR)?

Requests for conditional and final map revisions should be sent to the FEMA LOMC Clearinghouse. The address of the Clearinghouse can be found on page 42 and in the map revision application forms.

96. How long does it take to obtain a LOMA, LOMR, or PMR?

LOMAs and LOMR-Fs can generally be issued within 60 days. Times are specified from the receipt date of all technical or legal documentation. LOMRs take approximately 90 days for processing, but the number of days may increase if changes in flooding conditions are extensive or if BFEs increase.

97. If a LOMA, LOMR-F, or LOMR is issued by FEMA, will a lending institution automatically waive the flood insurance requirement?

Although FEMA may issue a LOMA, it is the lending institution's prerogative to require flood insurance beyond the provisions of the Flood Disaster Protection Act of 1973 and the National Flood Insurance Reform Act of 1994 before granting a loan or mortgage. Those seeking a LOMA should first confer with the affected lending institution to determine whether the institution will waive the requirement for flood insurance if a LOMA is issued. If it will, the policyholder may cancel flood insurance coverage and obtain a premium refund. If not, amending the NFIP map to remove the structure from the SFHA will generally lower the flood insurance premium.

Even if the lender waives the requirement of flood insurance, it is wise to keep coverage in force. History has proven that over 20 percent of all NFIP claims originate from areas mapped outside those considered at high risk.

98. If a LOMA, LOMR-F, or LOMR is granted and the lender waives the requirement for flood insurance, how can a flood insurance policy be canceled?

To cancel a flood insurance policy, the policyholder must supply a copy of the LOMA, LOMR-F, or LOMR and a waiver for the flood insurance purchase requirement from the lending institution to the insurance agent or broker who services the policy. A completed cancellation form with the LOMA, LOMR-F, or LOMR and the waiver must be submitted by the agent to the NFIP or the appropriate company.

When a LOMA, LOMR-F, or LOMR is issued and cancellation requested, the policyholder may be eligible for a refund of the premium paid for the current policy year only if no claim is pending and no claim has been paid during the current policy year.

Although a LOMA is issued and the lender has waived the requirement for flood insurance, it is wise to keep coverage in force. History has proven that over 20 percent of all NFIP flood claims originate from areas mapped outside those considered at high risk.

99. Why is the burden of proof on the person requesting a map change?

FEMA and its contractors exercise great care to ensure that analytical methods employed in FISs are scientifically and technically correct; engineering practices are followed to meet professional standards; and the results of the FIS are accurate. In making amendments and revisions to NFIP maps and reports, FEMA must adhere to the same engineering standards applied in preparing the effective maps and reports. Therefore, when requesting changes to NFIP maps, community officials and property owners are required to submit adequate supporting data.

100. Are fees assessed for map change requests submitted by community officials, developers, and property owners?

There are fees for some map change requests, but some are free. (To minimize the financial burden on policyholders while keeping the NFIP sustainable, FEMA implemented fees for reviewing and processing requests from some types of conditional and final map amendments and map revisions. Please see the fee schedule for more details.) The fee schedule for these requests is published in the *Federal Register* and applies to all types of requests except those that are specifically exempted in Section 72.5(c) of the NFIP Regulations. To get answers to fee-related questions, interested parties should either call the FMIX at 1-877-336-2627 or visit http://www.fema.gov/plan/prevent/fhm/frm_fees.shtm.

101. What is the purpose of the application/certification forms that are required for map change requests?

FEMA implemented the use of forms for requesting revisions or amendments to NFIP maps to provide a consistent and comprehensive process for requesters to follow. Experience has shown piecemeal submissions to be time-consuming and expensive. The forms help FEMA complete its review in less time.

102. How can someone obtain copies of the technical data used in preparing the published FEMA maps?

FEMA Engineering Library

The FEMA Engineering Library stores and provides technical and administrative support data related to the following:

- FEMA-contracted studies and restudies, including studies and restudies performed by participants in the FEMA Cooperating Technical Partners (CTP) program;

- Physical Map Revisions (PMRs);

- Conditional Letters of Map Amendment (CLOMAs);

- Letters of Map Amendment (LOMAs);

- Conditional Letters of Map Revision Based on Fill (CLOMR-Fs);

- Letters of Map Revision Based on Fill (LOMR-Fs);

- Conditional Letters of Map Revision (CLOMRs); *and*

- Letters of Map Revision (LOMRs).

To obtain technical and administrative data, a written request must be submitted to the FEMA Engineering Library at the address or fax number below. A Flood Insurance Study (FIS) Request Form, available at http://www.fema.gov/library/viewRecord.do?id=2223, includes additional information and fees for requesting Flood Insurance Study–related data.

> FEMA Engineering Library
> 847 S. Pickett St.
> Alexandria, VA 22304

> Phone: 1-877-336-2627
> Fax: 703-212-4090

FEMA LOMC Clearinghouse

As a result of numerous public requests for Flood Insurance Rate Map (FIRM) revisions and information about flood maps, FEMA has contracted with a professional engineering firm to provide these services to interested parties. Requests for conditional and final FIRM revisions should be sent to the FEMA LOMC Clearinghouse at the following address:

> LOMC Clearinghouse
> Attn: LOMC Manager
> 7390 Coca Cola Dr., Suite 204
> Hanover, MD 21076

For questions about FIRMs, the LOMA or LOMR-F, flood mapping procedures, or the map revision process, call 1-877-336-2627 toll-free and ask to speak with a "FEMA Flood Map Specialist."

Repetitive Loss Properties Strategy and FEMA Hazard Mitigation Grant Program

103. Is financial assistance available for NFIP policyholders to reduce their overall risk?

Yes, FEMA offers five hazard mitigation grant programs. Some grant programs are available only to NFIP policyholders.

104. What are the five hazard mitigation grant programs?

- Hazard Mitigation Grant Program (HMGP)
  (http://www.fema.gov/government/grant/hmgp/index.shtm)

- Pre-Disaster Mitigation Grant Program (PDM)
  (http://www.fema.gov/government/grant/pdm/index.shtm)

- Flood Mitigation Assistance Grant Program (FMA)
  (http://www.fema.gov/government/grant/fma/index.shtm)

- Repetitive Flood Claims Grant Program (RFC)
  (http://www.fema.gov/government/grant/rfc/index.shtm)

- Severe Repetitive Loss Grant Program (SRL)
  (http://www.fema.gov/government/grant/srl/index.shtm)

105. What is the Repetitive Loss Properties Strategy?

The primary objective of the Repetitive Loss Properties Strategy is to eliminate or reduce the damage to property and the disruption of life caused by repeated flooding of the same properties.

106. Is there a program available for severe repetitive loss properties?

A specific group of properties is identified and serviced separately from other NFIP policies by the Special Direct Facility (SDF). The properties include every NFIP-insured property that, since 1978 and regardless of any change(s) of ownership during that period, has experienced:

- At least four NFIP claim payments (including building and contents) over $5,000 each, and the cumulative amount of such claims payments exceeds $20,000; or

- For which at least two separate claims payments (building payments only) have been made with the cumulative amount of the building portion of such claims exceeding the market value of the building.

For both of the above options, at least two of the referenced claims must have occurred within any 10-year period, and must be greater than 10 days apart.

107. How is the loss history determined?

The loss history includes all flood claims paid on an insured property, regardless of any change(s) of ownership, since the building's construction or back to 1978 if the building was constructed before 1978. SRL properties are afforded coverage, whether new or renewal, only through the SDF.

108. How and when are affected property owners notified that their property is an SRL property?

At least 90 days before the policy renewal date, affected property owners and their flood insurance agents are sent notice by the Write Your Own (WYO) Company stating that the policy is ineligible for renewal through the WYO Program and offering renewal in the SDF. A follow-up notice is sent by the SDF 45 days before the renewal date.

109. How should an SRL policyholder respond after receiving such a renewal notice?

If the policyholder wishes to continue to have flood coverage, he or she should follow the renewal instructions provided by the SDF offer notice. He or she will not be able to renew the policy with the present WYO Company.

110. What procedures are available for property owners who believe that their property should not be included as an SRL property?

When a policyholder has documentation that the NFIP-insured property has not sustained the losses reported, a request for review may be presented, in writing, to the NFIP Bureau and Statistical Agent. All documentation to substantiate the review must be included with the request letter. The policy will remain in the SDF during the review.

111. What happens to an SRL property?

The appropriate FEMA Regional Office (see list beginning on page 43 in this book) provides information about the property to state and local floodplain management officials. States or communities may sponsor projects to mitigate flood losses to these properties or may be able to provide technical assistance on mitigation options.

112. What happens if a property owner agrees to undertake appropriate mitigation measures?

The property will be removed from the SRL validated list at the next renewal, and the policy then will be transferred from the SDF to the WYO Company that previously serviced the policy.

113. What kinds of mitigation measures are appropriate?

Depending on individual circumstances, appropriate mitigation measures commonly include elevating buildings above the level of the base flood, demolishing buildings, and removing buildings from the Special Flood Hazard Area (SFHA). Sometimes, mitigation takes the form of a local drainage-improvement project that meets NFIP standards.

114. If an NFIP policyholder who is an SRL property owner declines an official mitigation offer from FEMA, will his or her flood insurance premium increase?

Yes, his or her flood insurance premium will increase.

Presidential Disaster Declarations and the NFIP

115. What are examples of mitigation opportunities that may become available following a Presidential disaster declaration?

When major flooding disasters have affected a region, it is common for communities and individuals to consider relocation, acquisition, or elevation of flood-damaged structures. Property owners who sustained extensive damage are often very interested in avoiding the recurrence of such an experience. The feasibility of such mitigation projects must be established on a case-by-case basis. It is important for a flood insurance policyholder to be aware of these possibilities and contact local officials to learn as much as possible.

116. Are there any specific programs available associated with a Presidential disaster declaration to assist with mitigation?

Yes. The Hazard Mitigation Grant Program, authorized under Section 404 of the Robert T. Stafford Disaster Relief and Emergency Assistance Act, is FEMA's primary hazard mitigation program designed to assist states and communities in implementing long-term hazard mitigation measures following a major disaster declaration. States manage this program and may set state-specific project criteria. Individuals with questions should contact their local officials for more information. Through the Small Business Administration, loans may be available to qualifying applicants to assist with the costs of mitigation.

Due to the need to coordinate many activities following Presidential declarations, it is important for individual citizens to raise their questions and concerns about these post-disaster mitigation opportunities with their local community officials.

NFIP Program Information

General Information

For general program information or inquiries about the laws, regulations, or administrative policies related to the NFIP, write:

U.S. Department of Homeland Security
Federal Emergency Management Agency
Federal Insurance and Mitigation Administration
1800 S. Bell St.
Arlington, VA 20598-3010

For insurance questions, call local property insurance agents or brokers, or call the NFIP toll-free at 1-800-427-4661.

General program information may also be obtained at the following websites:

- FEMA on the Web
  http://www.fema.gov

- NFIP on the Web
  http://www.fema.gov/business/nfip
  http://www.floodsmart.gov

Specific Information and Resources

To order Flood Insurance Rate Maps, Digital Q3 Map Data, Flood Insurance Study reports, the NFIP *Community Status Book*, the NFIP *Flood Insurance Manual*, or other resources, contact the FEMA Map Service Center (MSC) at the address below or one of the toll-free numbers below, or order online at http://msc.fema.gov.

Federal Emergency Management Agency
FEMA Map Information eXchange (FMIX)
P.O. Box 1038
Jessup, MD 20794-1038

Phone: 1-877-336-2627
Fax: 1-800-358-9620

For information pertaining to hazard identification mapping and floodplain management, contact the local community administrator or the State NFIP Coordinating Agency (see list beginning on page 47).

FEMA LOMC Clearinghouse

As a result of numerous public requests for Flood Insurance Rate Map (FIRM) revisions and information about flood maps, FEMA has contracted with a professional engineering firm to provide these services to interested parties.

Requests for conditional and final revisions should be sent to the FEMA LOMC Clearinghouse at the following address:

> LOMC Clearinghouse
> 7390 Coca Cola Dr., Suite 204
> Hanover, MD 21076

For answers to questions about FIRMs, the LOMA or LOMR-F, flood mapping procedures, or the map revision process, call 1-877-336-2627 toll-free and ask to speak with a "FEMA Flood Map Specialist" or email the map specialist at FEMAMapSpecialist@riskmapcds.com.

FEMA Regional Offices

Region I – *Connecticut, Maine, Massachusetts, New Hampshire, Rhode Island, Vermont*

FEMA Region I Office
6th Floor
99 High St.
Boston, MA 02110

Phone: 617-956-7506

Region II – *New Jersey, New York*

FEMA Region II Office
Suite 1311
26 Federal Plaza
New York, NY 10278-0002

Phone: 212-680-3600

Region II (Caribbean) –
Puerto Rico, Virgin Islands

Physical Address
FEMA Region II Office
Caribbean Division
New San Juan Office Bldg.
159 Calle Chardon, 6th Floor
Hato Rey, PR 00918

Phone: 787-296-3500

Mailing Address
FEMA Region II Office
Caribbean Division
P.O. Box 70105
San Juan, PR 00936-0105

Region III – *Delaware, District of Columbia, Maryland, Pennsylvania, Virginia, West Virginia*

FEMA Region III Office
6th Floor
615 Chestnut St.
Philadelphia, PA 19106-4404

Phone: 215-931-5608

Region IV – *Alabama, Florida, Georgia, Kentucky, Mississippi, North Carolina, South Carolina, Tennessee*

FEMA Region IV Office
Suite 270
3003 Chamblee-Tucker Rd.
Atlanta, GA 30341

Phone: 770-220-5200

Region V – *Illinois, Indiana, Michigan, Minnesota, Ohio, Wisconsin*

FEMA Region V Office
536 S. Clark St., 6th Floor
Chicago, IL 60605

Phone: 312-408-5500

Region VI – *Arkansas, Louisiana, New Mexico, Oklahoma, Texas*

FEMA Region VI Office
Federal Regional Center
800 North Loop 288
Denton, TX 76201-3698

Phone: 940-898-5399

Region VII – *Iowa, Kansas, Missouri, Nebraska*

FEMA Region VII Office
9221 Ward Pkwy., Suite 300
Kansas City, MO 64114-3372

Phone: 816-283-7061

Region VIII – *Colorado, Montana, North Dakota, South Dakota, Utah, Wyoming*

FEMA Region VIII Office
Building 710
Denver Federal Center
P.O. Box 25267
Denver, CO 80225-0267

Phone: 303-235-4800

Region IX – *Arizona, California, Hawaii, Nevada; Territory of American Samoa, Territory of Guam, Commonwealth of the Northern Mariana Islands, Republic of the Marshall Islands, Federated States of Micronesia, Republic of Palau*

FEMA Region IX Office
Suite 1200
111 Broadway
Oakland, CA 94607-4052

Phone: 510-627-7100

Region X – *Alaska, Idaho, Oregon, Washington*

FEMA Region X Office
Federal Regional Center
130 228th St. SW
Bothell, WA 98021-9796

Phone: 425-487-4600

For the latest updates to this list, visit
http://www.fema.gov/about/contact/regions.shtm

NFIP Regional Offices

Region I – *Connecticut, Maine, Massachusetts, New Hampshire, Rhode Island, Vermont*

P.O. Box 2156
Merrimack, NH 03054

Phone: 603-423-0470
Fax: 603-423-0395

Region II – *New Jersey, New York, Puerto Rico, Virgin Islands*

P.O. Box 7342
Penndel, PA 19047

Phone: 267-560-5057
Fax: 267-560-5057

Region III – *Delaware, District of Columbia, Maryland, Pennsylvania, Virginia, West Virginia*

P.O. Box 7342
Penndel, PA 19047

Phone: 267-560-5057
Fax: 267-560-5057

Region IV – *Alabama, Georgia, Kentucky, Mississippi, North Carolina, South Carolina, Tennessee, Florida*

P.O. Box 1046
Zephyrhills, FL 33539-1049

Phone: 813-788-2624
Fax: 813-788-2710

Region IV – *Alabama, Georgia, Kentucky, Mississippi, North Carolina, South Carolina, Tennessee, Florida*

1000 Abernathy Rd. NE, Suite 900
Atlanta, GA 30328-5648

Phone: 770-614-0865

Region V – *Illinois, Indiana, Michigan, Minnesota, Ohio, Wisconsin*

100 S. Wacker Dr., Suite 500
Chicago, IL 60606

Phone: 312-596-6728
Fax: 312-939-4198

Region VI – *Arkansas, Louisiana, New Mexico, Oklahoma, Texas*

P.O. Box 561356
The Colony, TX 75056

Phone: 214-618-1092
Fax: 214-618-1092

Region VII – *Iowa, Kansas, Missouri, Nebraska*

8300 College Blvd., Suite 200
Overland Park, KS 66210

Phone: 913-344-1194
Fax: 913-344-1011

Region VIII – *Colorado, Montana, North Dakota, South Dakota, Utah, Wyoming*

999 18th St., Suite 900
Denver, CO 80202

Phone: 303-299-7873
Fax: 303-293-8585

Region IX – *Arizona, California, Guam, Hawaii, Nevada*

1333 Broadway, Suite 800
Oakland, CA 94612-1942

Phone: 510-874-1755
Fax: 510-874-3268

Region X – *Alaska, Idaho, Oregon, Washington*

1501 4th Ave., Suite 1400
Seattle, WA 98101

Phone: 206-438-2607
Fax: 510-874-3268

**For the latest updates to this list, visit
http://www.fema.gov/business/nfip/nfip_regions.shtm**

State NFIP Coordinating Agencies

Alabama

Alabama Department of Economic and
    Community Affairs
Office of Water Resources
P.O. Box 5690
Montgomery, AL 36103-5690

Phone: 334-353-0853
Fax: 334-242-0776

Alaska

Alaska Department of Community and
    Economic Development
550 W. 7th Ave., Suite 1770
Anchorage, AK 99501-3510

Phone: 907-269-4583
Fax: 907-269-4539

Arizona

Arizona Department of Water Resources
3550 N. Central Ave.
Phoenix, AZ 85012-2105

Phone: 602-771-8657
Fax: 602-771-8686

Arkansas

Arkansas Soil and Water Conservation
    Commission
101 E. Capitol Ave., Suite 350
Little Rock, AR 72201

Phone: 501-682-3969
Fax: 501-682-3991

California

California Department of Water Resources
2825 Watt Ave., Suite 100
Sacramento, CA 95821

Phone: 916-574-1475
Fax: 916-574-1478

Colorado

Colorado Water Conservation Board
1313 Sherman St., Room 721
Denver, CO 80203

Phone: 303-866-3441, Ext. 3215
Fax: 303-866-4474

Connecticut

NFIP State Coordinator
Connecticut Department of
    Environmental Protection
79 Elm St.
Hartford, CT 06106

Phone: 860-424-3537
Fax: 860-424-4075

Delaware

Delaware Department of Natural
    Resources
89 Kings Hwy.
Dover, DE 19901

Phone: 302-739-9921
Fax: 302-739-6724

District of Columbia

District Department of the Environment
Watershed Protection Division
51 N St., NE, 5th Floor, Room 5021
Washington, DC 20002

Phone: 202-535-2248 or 202-535-2240
Fax: 202-535-1364

Florida

Florida Division of Emergency
    Management
2555 Shumard Oak Blvd.
Tallahassee, FL 32399-2100

Phone: 850-922-4518

Georgia

Georgia Department of Natural Resources
7 Martin Luther King Dr., Suite 440
Atlanta, GA 30334

Phone: 404-656-6382
Fax: 404-656-6383

Hawaii

Hawaii Department of Land and
    Natural Resources
1151 Punchbowl St., Suite 221
Honolulu, HI 96809

Phone: 808-587-0267
Fax: 808-587-0283

Idaho

Idaho Department of Water Resources
322 E. Front St.
Boise, ID 83720

Phone: 208-287-4928
Fax: 208-287-6700

Illinois

Illinois Department of Natural Resources
One Natural Resources Way
Springfield, IL 62702-1271

Phone: 217-782-4428
Fax: 217-785-5014

Indiana

Indiana Division of Water
402 W. Washington St., Room W264
Indianapolis, IN 46204-2748

Phone: 317-234-1107
Fax: 317-233-4579

Iowa

Iowa Department of Natural Resources
Wallace State Office Bldg.
502 E. 9th St.
Des Moines, IA 50319

Phone: 515-281-8942
Fax: 515-281-8895

Kansas

Kansas Department of Agriculture
109 SW 9th St., 2nd Floor
Topeka, KS 66612-1283

Phone: 785-296-5440
Fax: 785-296-4835

Kentucky

Kentucky Division of Water
200 Fair Oaks Ln., 4th Floor
Frankfort, KY 40601

Phone: 502-564-3410
Fax: 502-564-9003

Louisiana

Louisiana Department of Transportation
    and Development
P.O. Box 94245
Baton Rouge, LA 70804-9425

Phone: 225-274-4354
Fax: 225-274-4351

Maine

Maine State Planning Office
38 State House Station, 184 State St.
Augusta, ME 04333-0038

Phone: 207-287-8063
Fax: 207-287-6489

Maryland

Maryland Department of the Environment
Water Management Administration
1800 Washington Blvd., Suite 430
Baltimore, MD 21230

Phone: 410-537-3775
Fax: 410-537-3751

Massachusetts

Massachusetts Department of
    Conservation and Recreation
251 Causeway St., Suite 800
Boston, MA 02114

Phone: 617-626-1406
Fax: 617-626-1349

Michigan
Michigan Department of Natural
    Resources and Environment
P.O. Box 30458
Lansing, MI 48909-7958

Phone: 517-335-3448
Fax: 517-373-9965

Minnesota
Minnesota Department of Natural
    Resources – Waters
500 Lafayette Rd.
St. Paul, MN 55155-4032

Phone: 651-259-5713
Fax: 651-296-0445

Mississippi
Mississippi Emergency Management
    Agency – Office of Mitigation
P.O. Box 5644
Pearl, MS 39208

Phone: 601-933-6884
Fax: 601-933-6805

Missouri
Missouri State Emergency Management
    Agency
P.O. Box 116
Jefferson City, MO 65102

Phone: 573-526-9141
Fax: 573-526-9198

Montana
Montana Floodplain Management Program
1424 9th Ave.
Helena, MT 59620-1601

Phone: 406-444-6654
Fax: 406-444-0533

Nebraska
Nebraska Department of
    Natural Resources
301 Centennial Mall South
Lincoln, NE 68509-4676

Phone: 402-471-3932
Fax: 402-471-2900

Nevada
Nevada Division of Water Resources
901 S. Stewart St., Suite 2002
Carson City, NV 89701

Phone: 775-684-2884
Fax: 775-684-2811

New Hampshire
Office of Energy and Planning
4 Chenell Dr.
Concord, NH 03301

Phone: 603-271-1762
Fax: 603-271-2615

New Jersey
New Jersey Department of
    Environmental Protection
P.O. Box 419
Trenton, NJ 08625

Phone: 609-984-0859/663-7297
Fax: 609-984-1908

New Mexico
Department of Homeland Security and
    Emergency Management
13 Bataan Blvd., P.O. Box 27111
Santa Fe, NM 87508

Phone: 505-476-9617
Fax: 505-471-9695

New York
New York Department of
    Environmental Conservation
625 Broadway
Albany, NY 12233-3504

Phone: 518-402-8146
Fax: 518-402-9029

North Carolina
North Carolina Division of
    Emergency Management
4719 Mail Service Ctr.
Raleigh, NC 27699-4719

Phone: 919-715-5711, Ext. 106
Fax: 919-715-0408

North Dakota
North Dakota State Water Commission
900 E. Boulevard Ave.
Bismarck, ND 58505-0850

Phone: 701-328-4898
Fax: 701-328-3747

Ohio
Ohio Department of Natural Resources
2045 Morse Rd., Bldg. B-2
Columbus, OH 43229-6693

Phone: 614-265-6752
Fax: 614-265-6767

Oklahoma
Oklahoma Water Resources Board
3800 N. Classen Blvd.
Oklahoma City, OK 73118

Phone: 918-581-2924
Fax: 918-581-2754

Oregon
Department of Land Conservation and
    Development
635 Capitol St., NE, Suite 150
Salem, OR 97301-2540

Phone: 503-373-0050 x250
Fax: 503-375-5518

Pennsylvania
Department of Community and Economic
    Development
Commonwealth Keystone Building
400 North St., 4th Floor
Harrisburg, PA 17120-0225

Phone: 717-720-7396
Fax: 717-783-1402

Puerto Rico
Puerto Rico Planning Board
P.O. Box 41119 – Minillas Govt. Center
Santurce, PR 00940-1119

Phone: 787-727-4444

Rhode Island
Rhode Island Emergency Management
    Agency
645 New London Ave.
Cranston, RI 02920

Phone: 401-462-7048
Fax: 401-944-1891

South Carolina
South Carolina Department of Natural
    Resources
1000 Assemply St., Suite 345C
P.O. Box 167
Columbia, SC 29201

Phone: 803-734-9120
Fax: 803-734-9106

South Dakota
South Dakota Division of Emergency
    Management
118 W. Capitol Ave.
Pierre, SD 57501

Phone: 605-773-3238

Tennessee
Tennessee Department of Economic and
    Community Development
312 8th Ave. N., TN Tower Bldg.,
    10th Floor
Nashville, TN 37243-0405

Phone: 615-741-2211
Fax: 615-741-0607

Texas
Texas Water Development Board
1700 N. Congress Ave.
P.O. Box 13231
Austin, TX 78711-3231

Phone: 512-463-3509
Fax: 512-475-2053

Utah
Utah Division of Homeland Security
Box 141710
1110 State Office Bldg.
Salt Lake City, UT 84114

Phone: 801-538-3332
Fax: 801-538-3772

Vermont
Water Quality Division – River
    Management Program
Vermont Department of
    Environmental Conservation
103 S. Main St., Bldg. 10N
Waterbury, VT 05671

Phone: 802-241-1554

Virginia
Virginia Department of Conservation
    and Recreation
Division of Dam Safety and
    Floodplain Management
203 Governor St., Suite 210
Richmond, VA 23219-2094

Phone: 804-371-6135
Fax: 804-371-2630

Virgin Islands
Virgin Island Planning and
    Natural Resources
C.E. King Airport, Termnl. Bldg., 2nd Floor
St. Thomas, VI 00802

Phone: 340-774-3320
Fax: 340-775-5706

Washington
Washington Department of Ecology
P.O. Box 47600
Olympia, WA 98504-7600

Phone: 360-407-6796
Fax: 360-407-6902

West Virginia
West Virginia Office of
    Emergency Services
1900 Kanawha Blvd., Cap Bldg. 1,
    Rm. EB-80
Charleston, WV 25305-0360

Phone: 304-957-2571
Fax: 304-965-3216

Wisconsin
Wisconsin Department of
    Natural Resources
101 S. Webster
Madison, WI 53702

Phone: 608-266-3093

Wyoming
Wyoming Office of Homeland Security
Herschler Bldg. 1E
122 W. 25th St.
Cheyenne, WY 82002

Phone: 307-777-4910
Fax: 307-635-6017

For the latest updates to this list, visit
the website of the Association of State Floodplain Managers at
http://www.floods.org/statepocs/stcoor.asp

Additional Resources

The following publications on flood-related subjects are available at no charge from the Federal Emergency Management Agency. Ordering information is provided at the end of this list.

FEMA 54: *Elevated Residential Structures* – Covers proper design and construction methods for elevated homes.

FEMA 55: *Coastal Construction Manual* – Provides a comprehensive approach to sensible development in coastal areas based on guidance from over 200 experts in building science, coastal hazard mitigation, and building codes and regulatory requirements.

FEMA 85: *Protecting Manufactured Homes from Floods and Other Hazards* – Reflects the requirements of the most current codes and standards, and provides a best practices approach in reducing damages from natural hazards. Also recommends several multi-hazard resistant foundation designs.

FEMA 186: *Mandatory Purchase of Flood Insurance Guidelines* – Presents an overview of the Flood Disaster Protection Act of 1973 and the National Flood Insurance Reform Act of 1994, which amends the Act of 1973. Explains the applicable statutes or regulations.

FEMA 213: *Answers to Questions About Substantially Damaged Buildings* – Provides guidance for determining whether a building has been substantially damaged.

FEMA 234: *Repairing Your Flooded Home* – Gives step-by-step advice to clean up, rebuild, and get help after a flood.

FEMA 259: *Engineering Principles and Practices for Retrofitting Flood-prone Residential Buildings* – Provides engineering design and economic guidance to engineers, architects, and local code officials about what constitutes technically feasible and cost-effective retrofitting measures for floodprone residential structures.

FEMA 265: *Managing Floodplain Development in Approximate Zone A Areas* – A guide for use by community officials, property owners, developers, surveyors, and engineers who may need to determine Base Flood Elevations (BFEs) in Special Flood Hazard Areas (SFHAs) designated as approximate Zone A on Flood Insurance Rate Maps (FIRMs).

FEMA 268: *Protecting Floodplain Resources* – A guidebook for officials and citizens at the local level on protecting natural resources in floodplains. Offers suggestions for creating strategies for wisely managing floodplain natural resources.

FEMA 301: *Increased Cost of Compliance Coverage: Guidance for State and Local Officials* – Provides information on the Increased Cost of Compliance coverage and how it relates to communities' administration of floodplain management laws or ordinances following a flooding event.

FEMA 347: *Above the Flood: Elevating your Flood Prone Home* – Shows how flood-prone houses in south Florida were elevated above the 100-year flood level following Hurricane Andrew. Alternative elevation techniques are also demonstrated.

FEMA 348: *Protecting Building Utilities from Flood Damage* – Provides assistance in the construction of buildings with building utility systems that are designed and built so that the buildings can be re-occupied and fully operational as soon as electricity and sewer and water are restored to the neighborhood.

FEMA 480: *Floodplain Management Requirements: A Study Guide and Desk Reference for Local Officials* – Provides guidance on how to handle many of the issues that will help floodplain managers explain the requirements to citizens of your community. It can also be used to study for the exam for the Association of State Floodplain Manager's (ASFPM) Certified Floodplain Manager designation.

FEMA 499: *Home Builder's Guide to Coastal Construction* – Presents information aimed at improving the performance of buildings subject to flood and wind forces in coastal environments.

FEMA 551: *Selecting Appropriate Mitigation Measures for Flood Prone Structures* – Provides guidance to community officials for developing mitigation projects that reduce or eliminate identified risks for flood-prone structures.

FEMA 758: *Substantial Improvement/Substantial Damage Desk Reference* – Provides practical guidance and suggested procedures to implement the NFIP requirements for Substantial Improvement/Substantial Damage.

FEMA 762: *Local Officials Guide for Coastal Construction* – Provides building officials with an understanding of the connection between National Flood Insurance Program (NFIP) guidelines, the International Building Code, and the International Residential Code.

FEMA 784: *Substantial Damage Estimator* – Provides assistance to state and local officials in estimating building value and costs to repair for residential and non-residential buildings.

MitDiv 2: *Answers to Questions About the NFIP* (this book) – Provides nontechnical answers to questions frequently asked about the National Flood Insurance Program by community officials, present and prospective policyholders, real estate agents, lenders, and others.

MitDiv 12: *Appeals, Revisions, and Amendments to Flood Insurance Maps: A Guide for Community Officials* – Provides detailed information on submittal and processing requirements for appeals, comments received during appeal periods, map revisions, map amendments, conditional map revisions and amendments, flood protection restoration determinations, adequate progress determinations, and Letters of Determination Review.

To order most FEMA and Mitigation Division publications about the NFIP, write, phone, or fax the FEMA Distribution Center (see below). You can download the Public Awareness Materials Order Form on the Web at http://www.fema.gov/library/viewRecord.do?id=1400.

FEMA Distribution Center
P.O. Box 430
Buckeystown, MD 21717

Telephone: 800-480-2520
Fax: 240-699-0525

Please cite both the publication number and title when ordering.

To obtain the *CRS Coordinator's Manual*, information pertaining to the Community Rating System (CRS), and software for completing the CRS application, write, phone, or fax your request to:

NFIP/CRS
P.O. Box 501016
Indianapolis, IN 46250-1016

Phone: 317-848-2898
Fax: 317-848-3578

CRS information can also be found on the Web at http://www.fema.gov/business/nfip/crs.shtm